CHEQUE REGISTER LOG

Business	
Address	
Log#	
Start Date	
End Date	

Notes

Number	Date	Transaction	Withdrawal	√	Depo sit	$	

Number	Date	Transaction	Withdrawal	√	Depo sit	$	

Number	Date	Transaction	Withdrawal	√	Depo sit	$

Number	Date	Transaction	Withdrawal		√	Depo sit		$	

Number	Date	Transaction	Withdrawal	√	Depo sit	$

Number	Date	Transaction	Withdrawal	√	Depo sit	$

Number	Date	Transaction	Withdrawal	√	Depo sit	$	

Number	Date	Transaction	Withdrawal	√	Depo sit	$

Number	Date	Transaction	Withdrawal	√	Depo sit	$

Number	Date	Transaction	Withdrawal	√	Depo sit	$	

Number	Date	Transaction	Withdrawal	√	Depo sit	$

Number	Date	Transaction	Withdrawal	√	Depo sit	$

Number	Date	Transaction	Withdrawal		√	Depo sit		$	

Number	Date	Transaction	Withdrawal	√	Depo sit	$	

Number	Date	Transaction	Withdrawal	√	Depo sit	$	

Number	Date	Transaction	Withdrawal	√	Depo sit	$

Number	Date	Transaction	Withdrawal	√	Depo sit	$

Number	Date	Transaction	Withdrawal	√	Depo sit	$

Number	Date	Transaction	Withdrawal	√	Depo sit	$	

Number	Date	Transaction	Withdrawal	√	Depo sit	$

Number	Date	Transaction	Withdrawal	√	Depo sit	$

Number	Date	Transaction	Withdrawal	√	Depo sit	$

Number	Date	Transaction	Withdrawal	√	Depo sit	$

Number	Date	Transaction	Withdrawal	√	Depo sit	$

Number	Date	Transaction	Withdrawal	√	Depo sit	$

Number	Date	Transaction	Withdrawal	√	Depo sit	$	

Number	Date	Transaction	Withdrawal	√	Depo sit	$

Number	Date	Transaction	Withdrawal	√	Depo sit	$	

Number	Date	Transaction	Withdrawal	√	Depo sit	$	

Number	Date	Transaction	Withdrawal		√	Depo sit		$	

Number	Date	Transaction	Withdrawal	√	Depo sit	$	

Number	Date	Transaction	Withdrawal	√	Depo sit	$	

Number	Date	Transaction	Withdrawal	√	Depo sit	$	

Number	Date	Transaction	Withdrawal	√	Depo sit	$	

Number	Date	Transaction	Withdrawal	√	Depo sit	$	

Number	Date	Transaction	Withdrawal	√	Depo sit	$

Number	Date	Transaction	Withdrawal		√	Depo sit		$	

Number	Date	Transaction	Withdrawal	√	Depo sit	$	

Number	Date	Transaction	Withdrawal	√	Depo sit	$

Number	Date	Transaction	Withdrawal	√	Depo sit	$	

Number	Date	Transaction	Withdrawal	√	Depo sit	$	

Number	Date	Transaction	Withdrawal	√	Depo sit	$

Number	Date	Transaction	Withdrawal	√	Depo sit	$	

Number	Date	Transaction	Withdrawal	√	Depo sit	$

Number	Date	Transaction	Withdrawal	√	Depo sit	$

Number	Date	Transaction	Withdrawal	√	Depo sit	$

Number	Date	Transaction	Withdrawal	√	Depo sit	$	

Number	Date	Transaction	Withdrawal	√	Depo sit	$

Number	Date	Transaction	Withdrawal	√	Depo sit	$	

Number	Date	Transaction	Withdrawal	√	Depo sit	$

Number	Date	Transaction	Withdrawal	√	Depo sit	$	

Number	Date	Transaction	Withdrawal	√	Depo sit	$

Number	Date	Transaction	Withdrawal	√	Depo sit	$	

Number	Date	Transaction	Withdrawal	√	Depo sit	$

Number	Date	Transaction	Withdrawal	√	Depo sit	$

Number	Date	Transaction	Withdrawal	√	Depo sit	$

Number	Date	Transaction	Withdrawal	√	Depo sit	$	

Number	Date	Transaction	Withdrawal	√	Depo sit	$	

Number	Date	Transaction	Withdrawal	√	Depo sit	$	

Number	Date	Transaction	Withdrawal	√	Depo sit	$

Number	Date	Transaction	Withdrawal	√	Depo sit	$	

Number	Date	Transaction	Withdrawal	√	Depo sit	$	

Number	Date	Transaction	Withdrawal	√	Depo sit	$

Number	Date	Transaction	Withdrawal	√	Depo sit	$

Number	Date	Transaction	Withdrawal		√	Depo sit		$	

Number	Date	Transaction	Withdrawal	√	Depo sit	$

Number	Date	Transaction	Withdrawal	√	Depo sit	$	

Number	Date	Transaction	Withdrawal	√	Depo sit	$

Number	Date	Transaction	Withdrawal	√	Depo sit	$

Number	Date	Transaction	Withdrawal	√	Depo sit	$	

Number	Date	Transaction	Withdrawal	√	Depo sit	$	

Number	Date	Transaction	Withdrawal	√	Depo sit	$	

Number	Date	Transaction	Withdrawal	√	Depo sit	$

Number	Date	Transaction	Withdrawal	√	Depo sit	$	

Number	Date	Transaction	Withdrawal	√	Depo sit	$	

Number	Date	Transaction	Withdrawal	√	Depo sit	$

Number	Date	Transaction	Withdrawal	√	Depo sit	$

Number	Date	Transaction	Withdrawal	√	Depo sit	$	

Number	Date	Transaction	Withdrawal		√	Depo sit		$	

Number	Date	Transaction	Withdrawal	√	Depo sit	$

Number	Date	Transaction	Withdrawal	√	Depo sit	$

Number	Date	Transaction	Withdrawal		√	Depo sit		$	

Number	Date	Transaction	Withdrawal	√	Depo sit	$	

Number	Date	Transaction	Withdrawal	√	Depo sit	$

Number	Date	Transaction	Withdrawal	√	Depo sit	$

Number	Date	Transaction	Withdrawal	√	Depo sit	$	

Number	Date	Transaction	Withdrawal	√	Depo sit	$

Number	Date	Transaction	Withdrawal	√	Depo sit	$

Number	Date	Transaction	Withdrawal	√	Depo sit	$

Number	Date	Transaction	Withdrawal	√	Depo sit	$	

Number	Date	Transaction	Withdrawal	√	Depo sit	$

Number	Date	Transaction	Withdrawal	√	Depo sit	$

Number	Date	Transaction	Withdrawal	√	Depo sit	$

Number	Date	Transaction	Withdrawal	√	Depo sit	$

Number	Date	Transaction	Withdrawal	√	Depo sit	$	

Number	Date	Transaction	Withdrawal	√	Deposit	$

Number	Date	Transaction	Withdrawal	√	Depo sit	$	

Number	Date	Transaction	Withdrawal	√	Depo sit	$

Number	Date	Transaction	Withdrawal	√	Depo sit	$	

Number	Date	Transaction	Withdrawal	√	Depo sit	$

Number	Date	Transaction	Withdrawal	√	Depo sit	$	

Number	Date	Transaction	Withdrawal		√	Depo sit		$